SAINT SAYINGS

About

The Eucharist

Illustrated by Beth Ann Ramos

For Beckett, in celebration of your
First Holy Communion.
I am so proud of you, and I will always
love you more than the world.
~Mom

Illustrated by Beth Ann Ramos
Published by Good Day Books
First Edition

Learn more at www.bethannramos.com.

good day
BOOKS

A Gift For:

_____

John 6:53-58

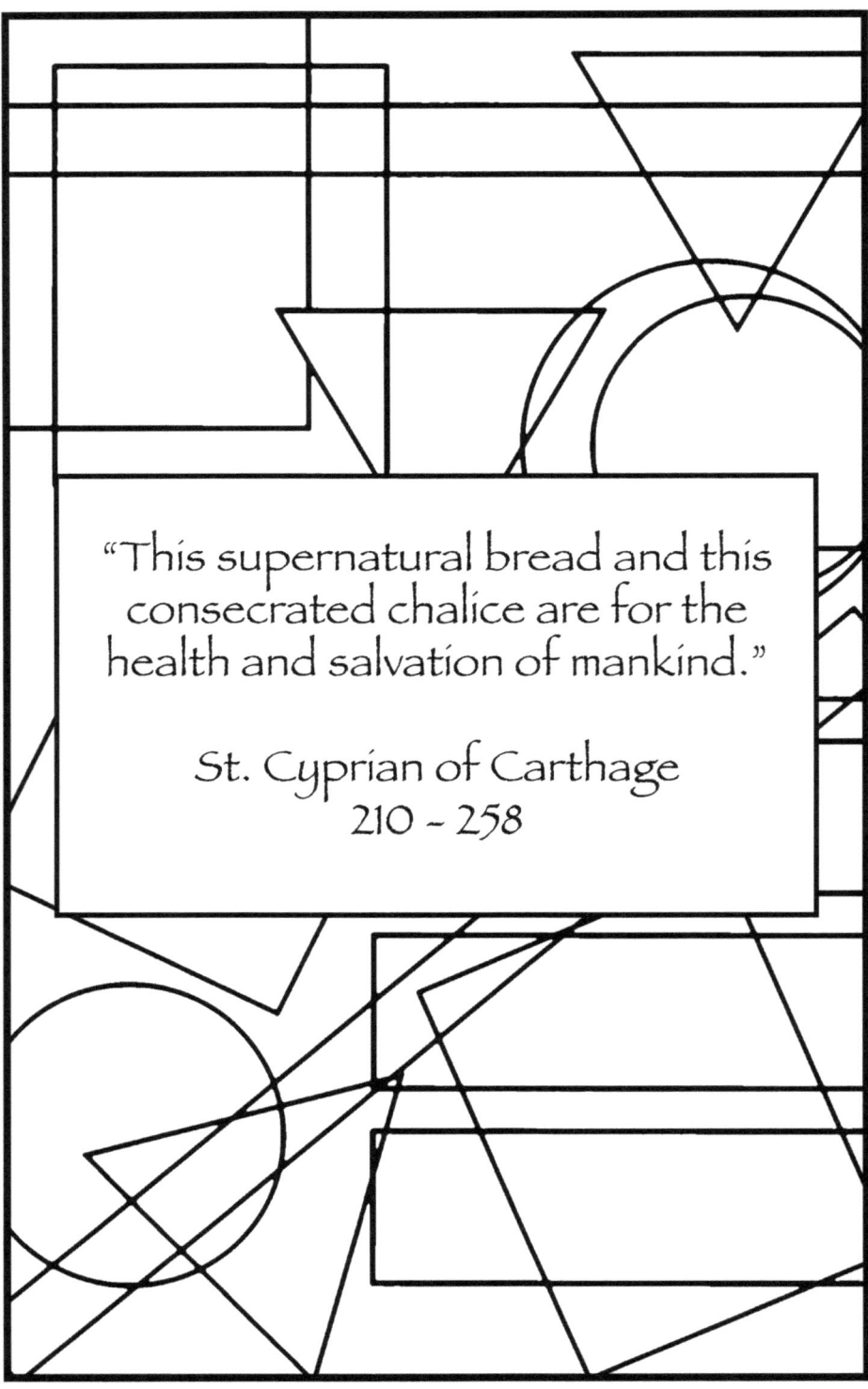

"This supernatural bread and this consecrated chalice are for the health and salvation of mankind."

St. Cyprian of Carthage
210 - 258

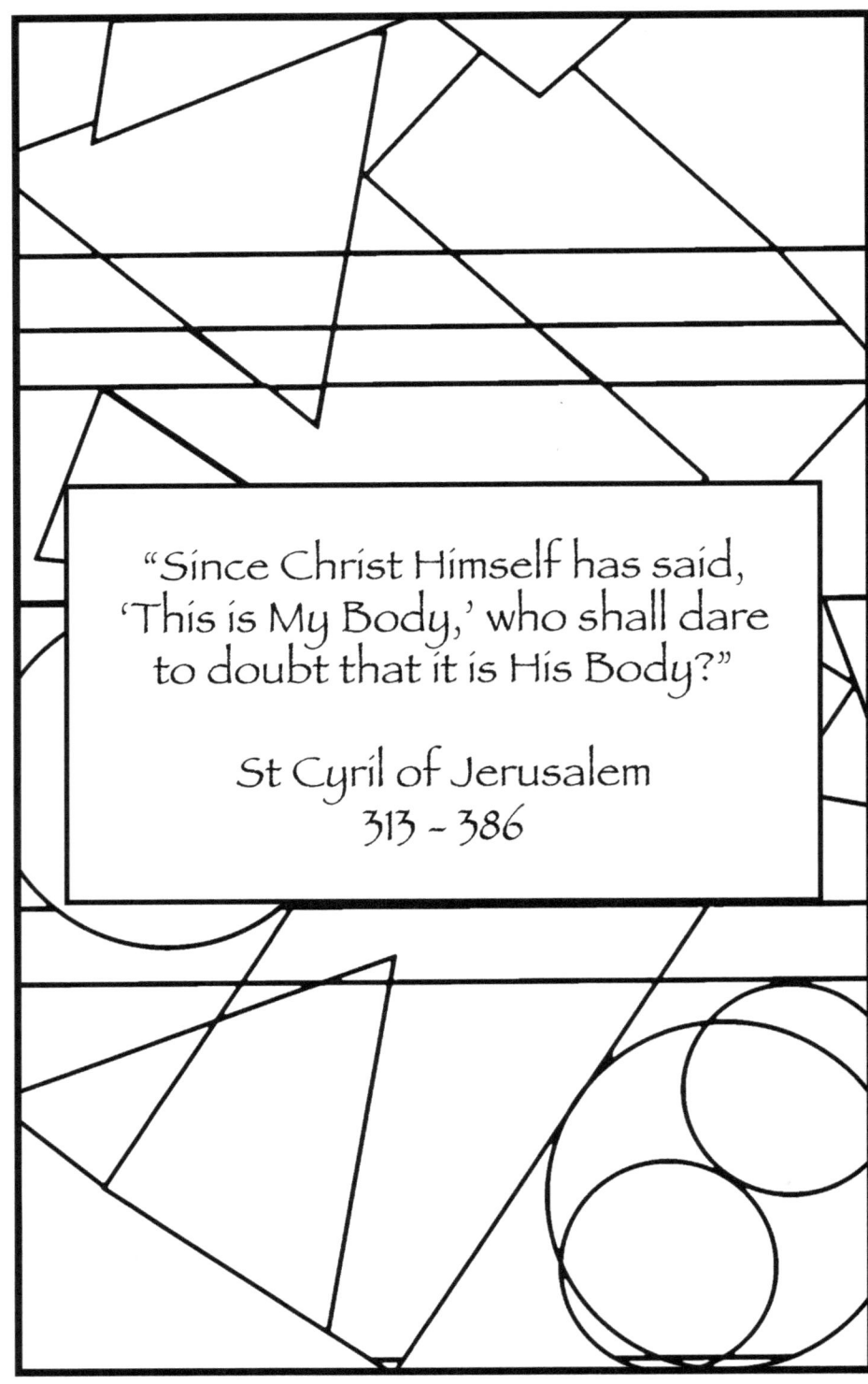

"Since Christ Himself has said, 'This is My Body,' who shall dare to doubt that it is His Body?"

St Cyril of Jerusalem
313 - 386

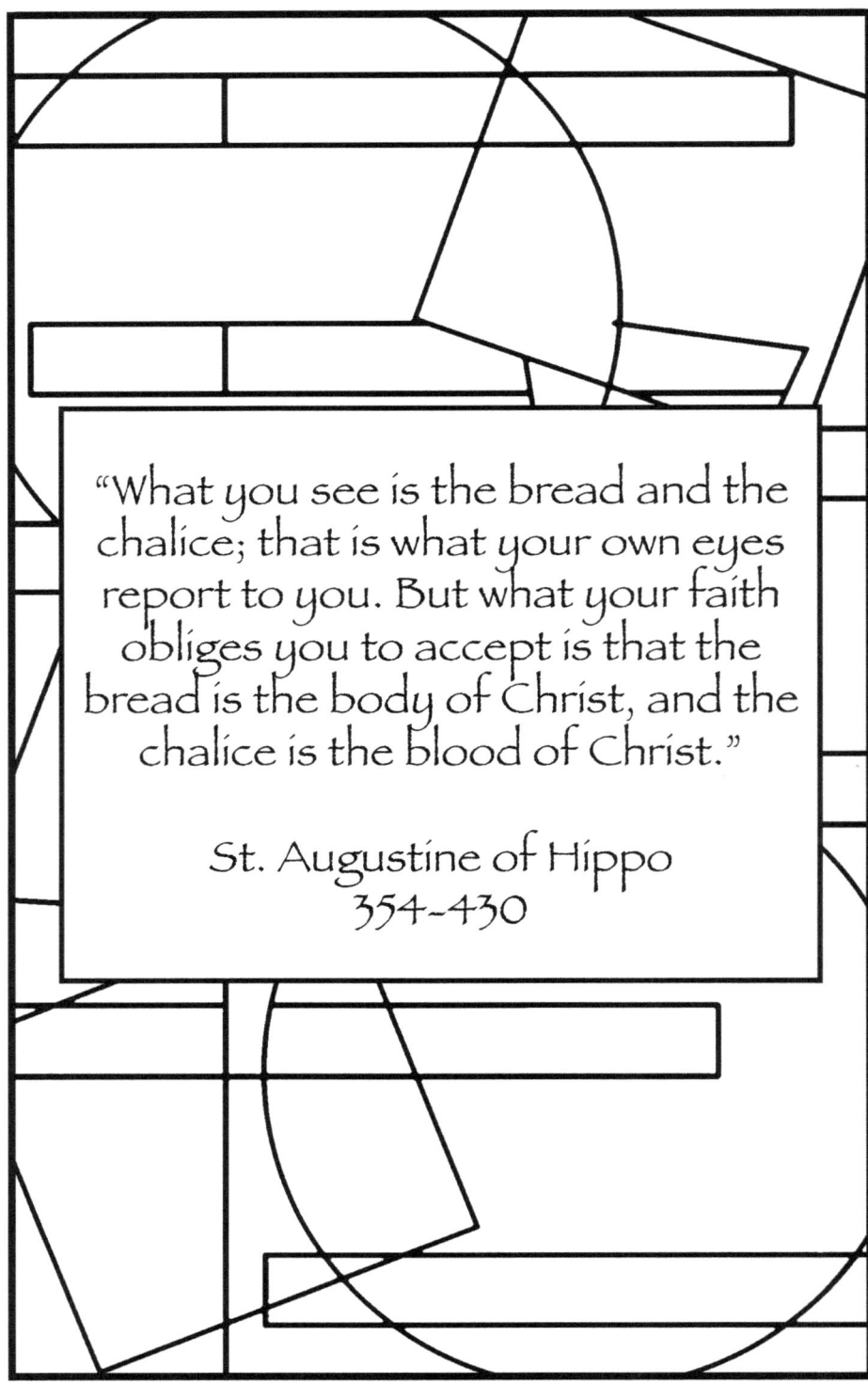

"What you see is the bread and the chalice; that is what your own eyes report to you. But what your faith obliges you to accept is that the bread is the body of Christ, and the chalice is the blood of Christ."

St. Augustine of Hippo
354-430

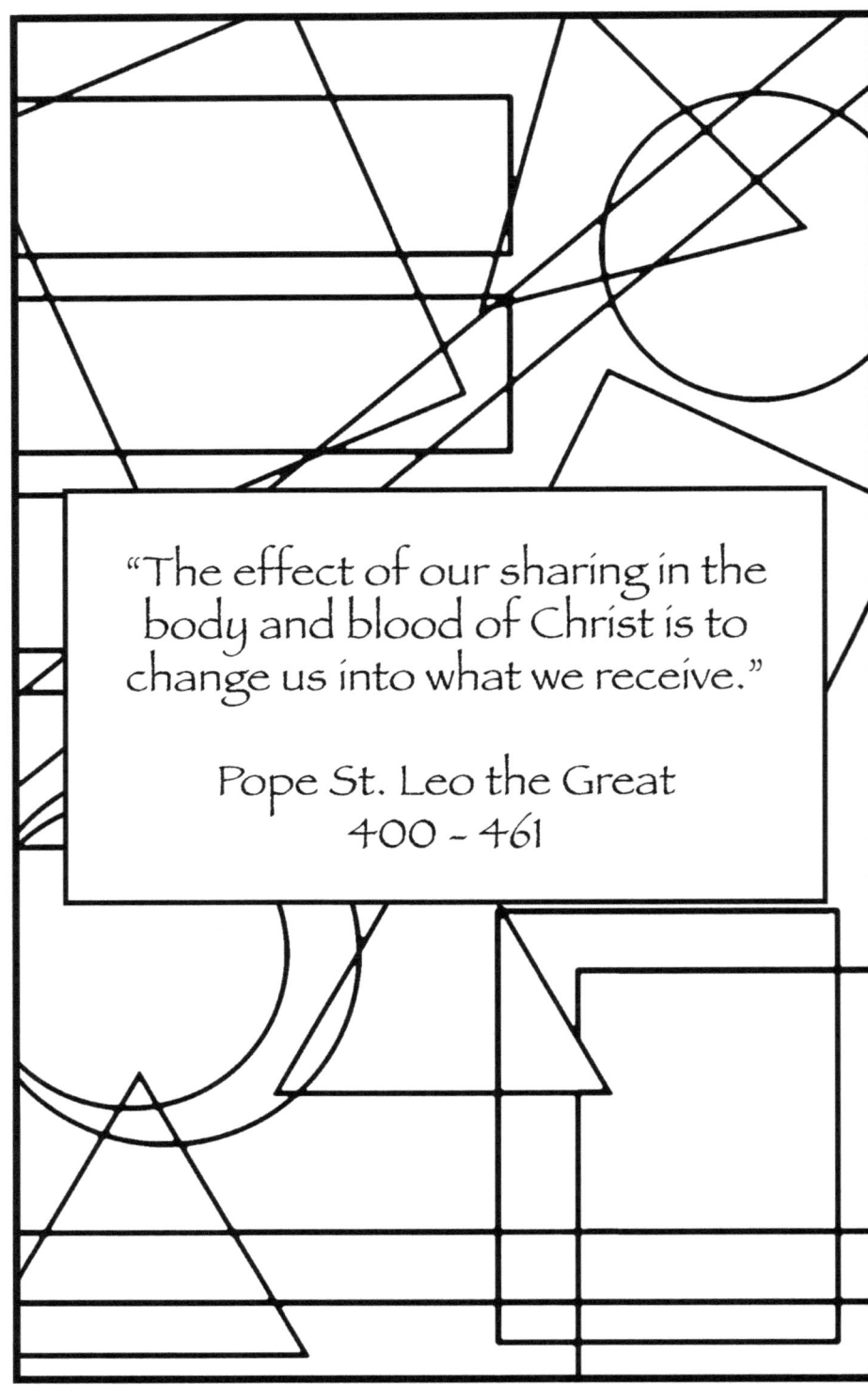

"The effect of our sharing in the body and blood of Christ is to change us into what we receive."

Pope St. Leo the Great
400 - 461

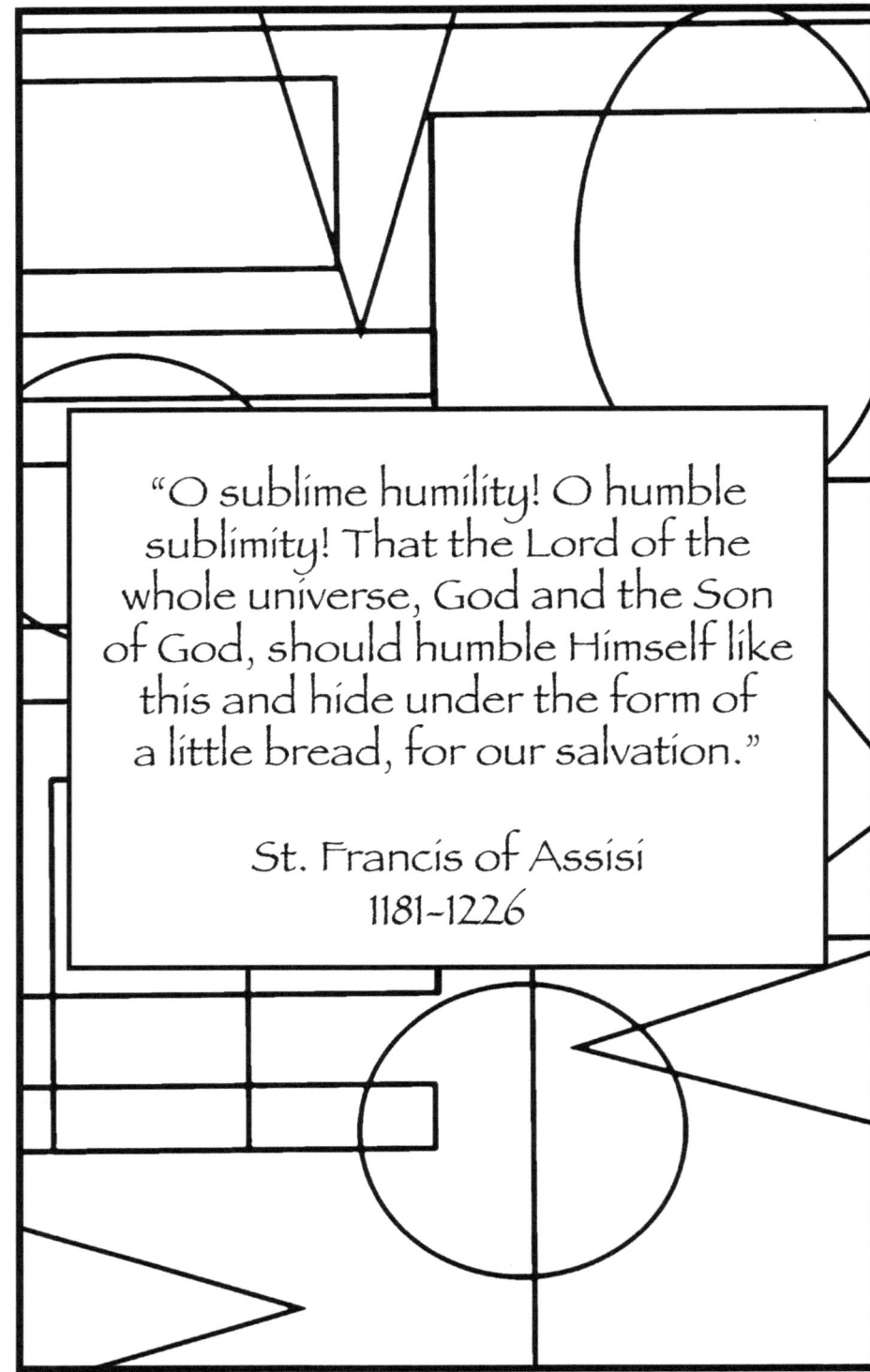

"O sublime humility! O humble sublimity! That the Lord of the whole universe, God and the Son of God, should humble Himself like this and hide under the form of a little bread, for our salvation."

St. Francis of Assisi
1181–1226

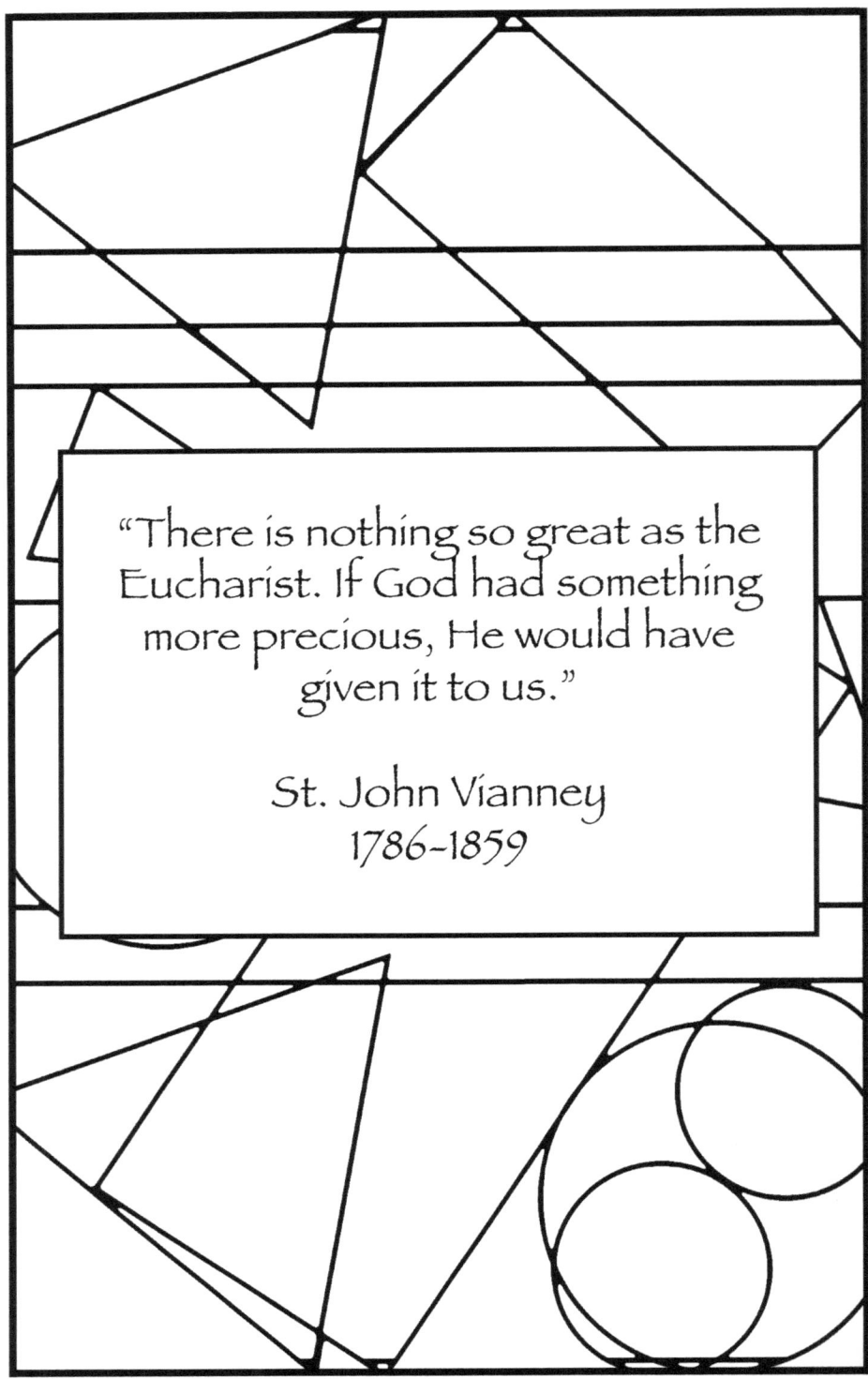

"There is nothing so great as the Eucharist. If God had something more precious, He would have given it to us."

St. John Vianney
1786-1859

"Holy communion is the shortest
and safest way to Heaven."

St. Pope Pius X
1835-1914

"Go often to Holy Communion.
Go very often!
This is your one remedy."

St Thérèse of Lisieux
1837–1897

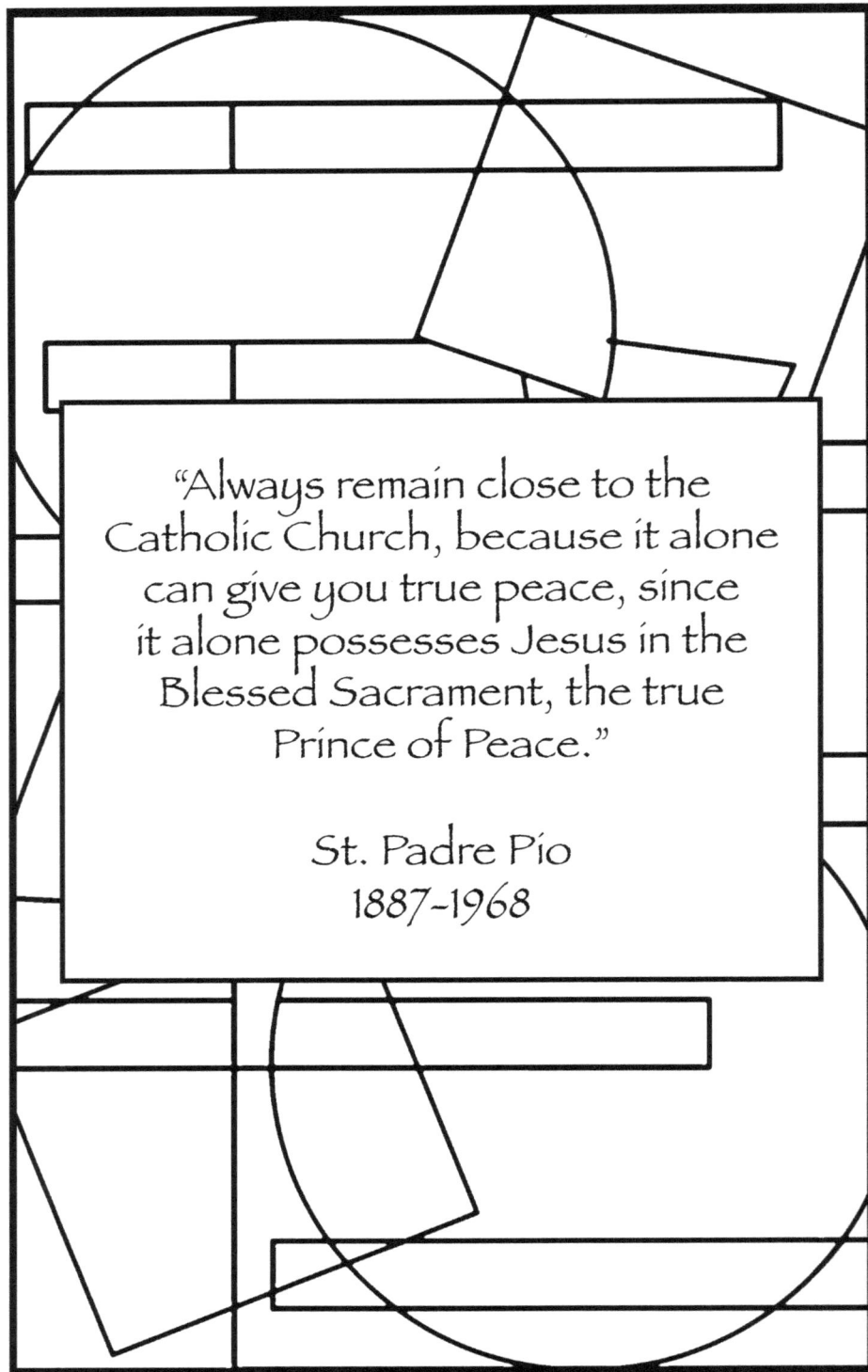

"Always remain close to the Catholic Church, because it alone can give you true peace, since it alone possesses Jesus in the Blessed Sacrament, the true Prince of Peace."

St. Padre Pio
1887-1968

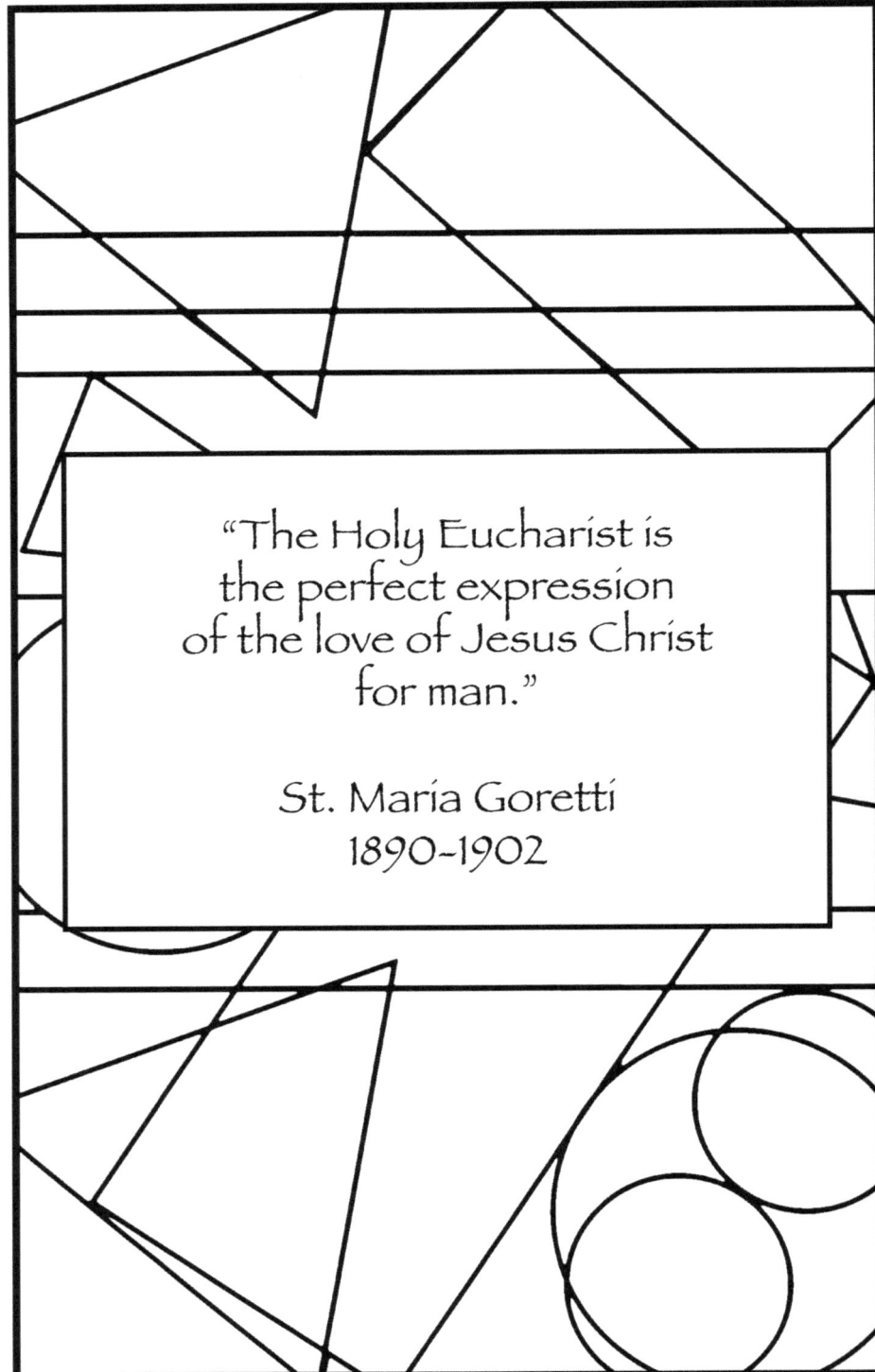

"The Holy Eucharist is
the perfect expression
of the love of Jesus Christ
for man."

St. Maria Goretti
1890-1902

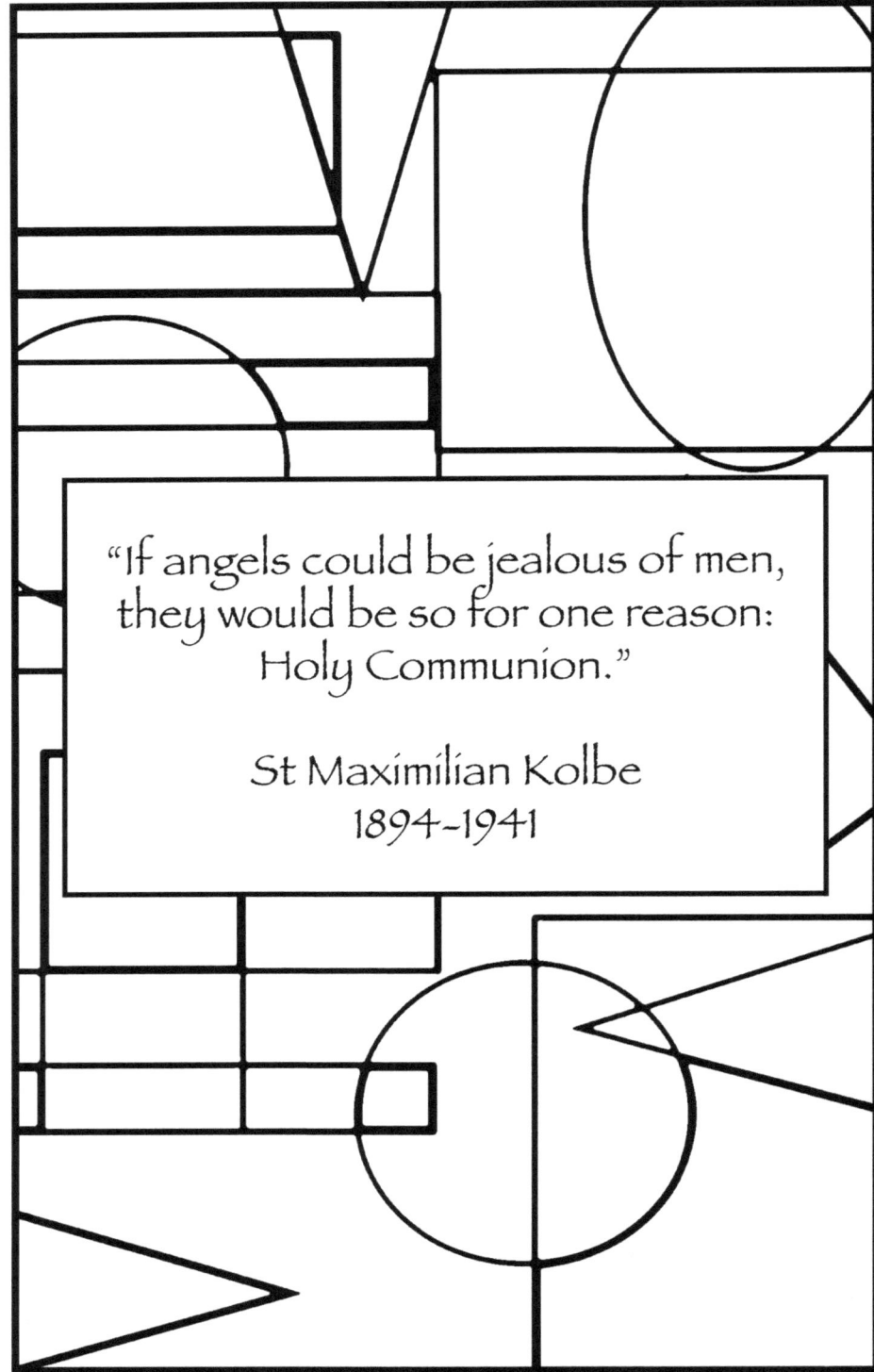

"If angels could be jealous of men, they would be so for one reason: Holy Communion."

St Maximilian Kolbe
1894–1941

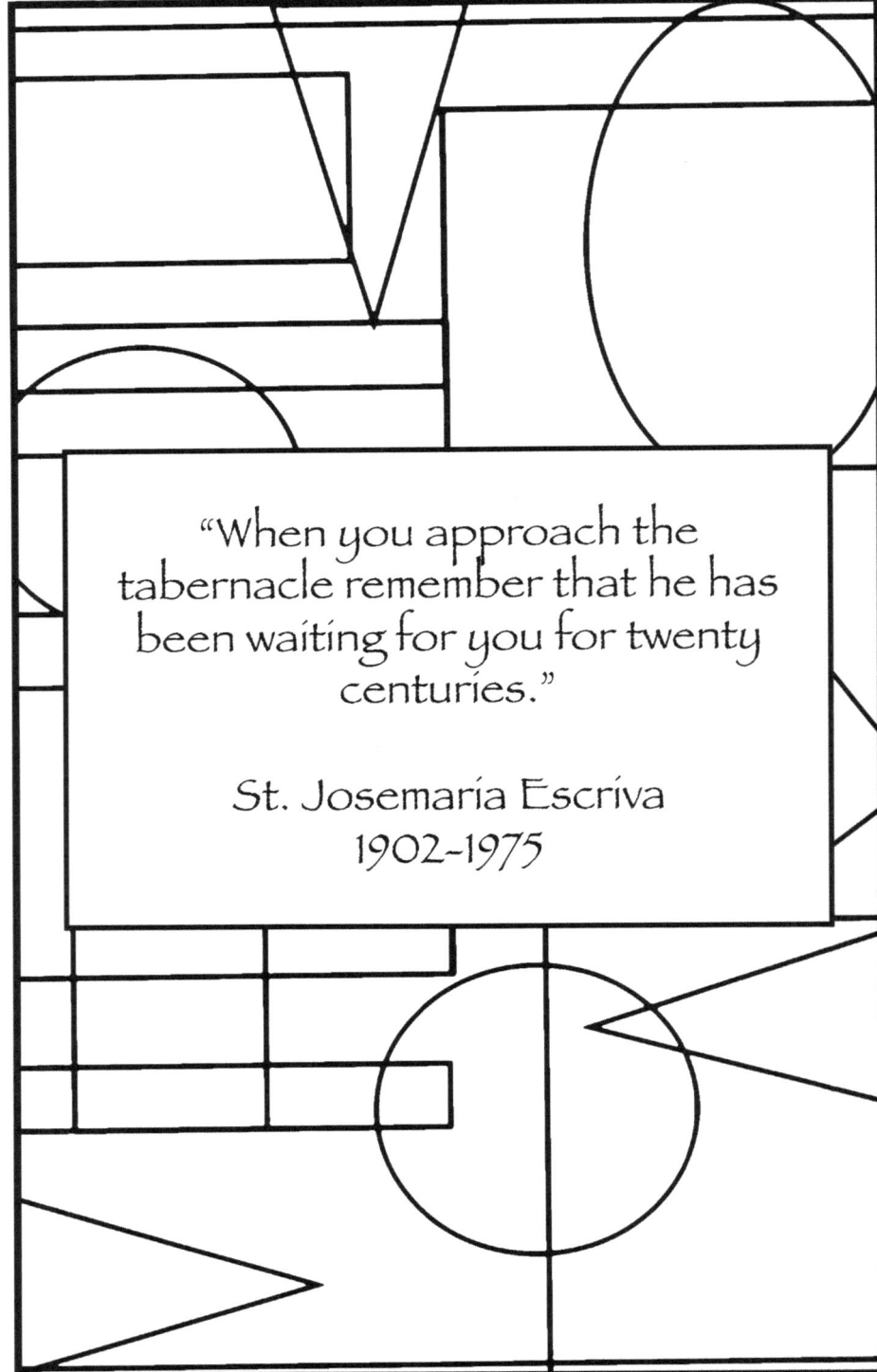

"When you approach the tabernacle remember that he has been waiting for you for twenty centuries."

St. Josemaria Escriva
1902-1975

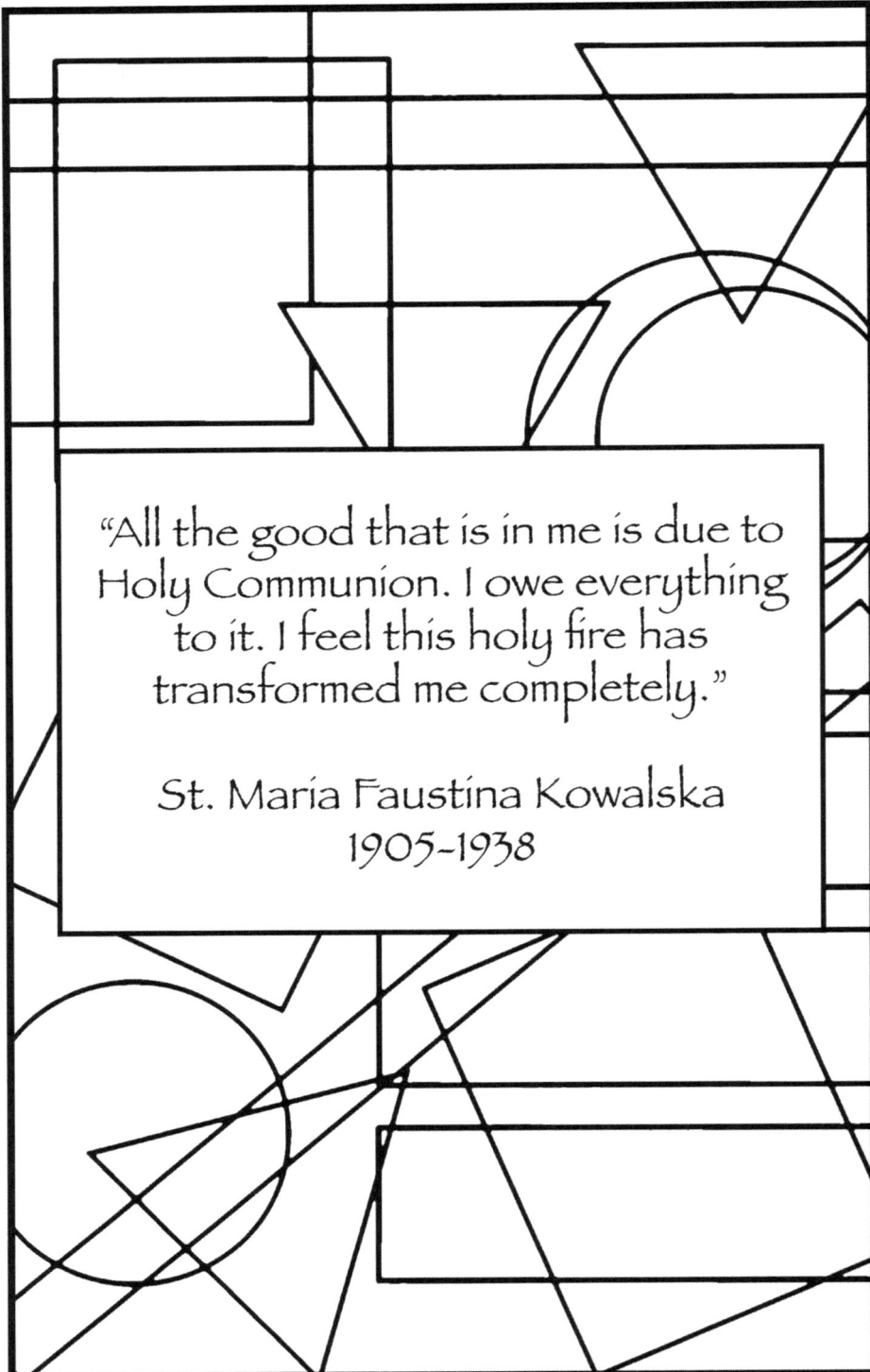

"All the good that is in me is due to Holy Communion. I owe everything to it. I feel this holy fire has transformed me completely."

St. Maria Faustina Kowalska
1905-1938

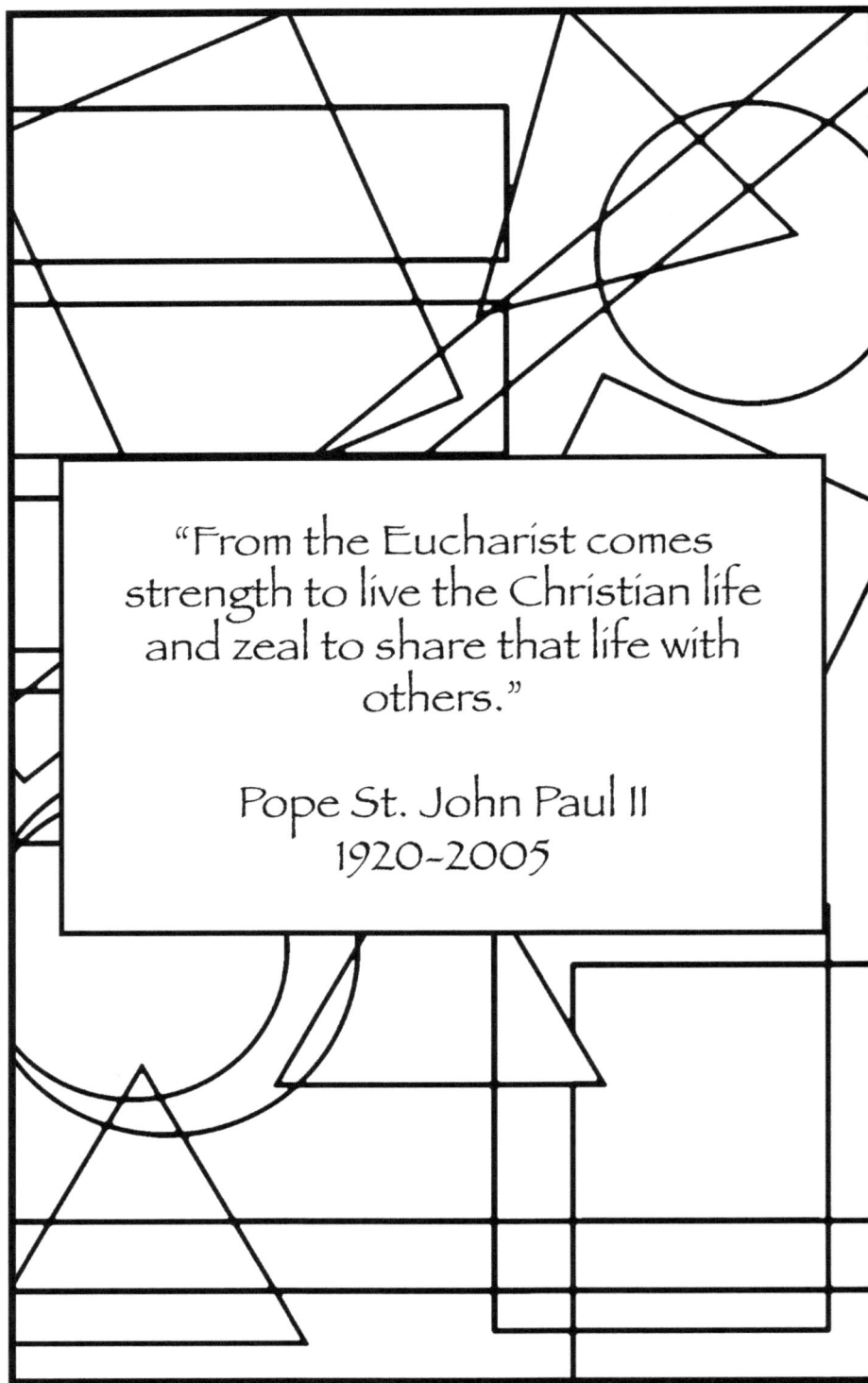

"From the Eucharist comes strength to live the Christian life and zeal to share that life with others."

Pope St. John Paul II
1920-2005

Also Available

Free activities and coloring pages available at:
www.bethannramos.com/eucharist

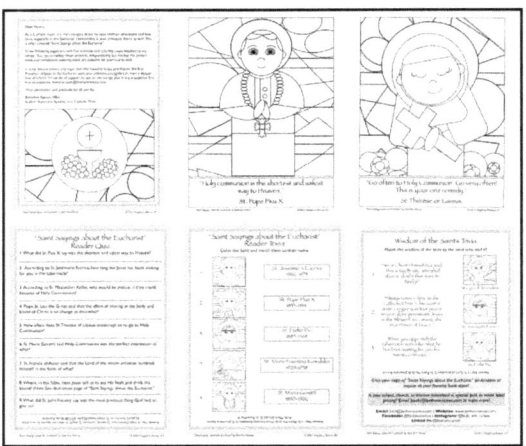

Email books@bethannramos.com
to inquire about bulk or white label pricing for
your school, church, or diocese!

www.ingramcontent.com/pod-product-compliance
Lightning Source LLC
Chambersburg PA
CBHW051651120626
46551CB00015B/2317